To Christopher
with thanks

James Strecker
1990

BOOKS BY JAMES STRECKER

Bones to Bury
Pas de Vingt (with Harold Town)
Corkscrew
Routes (with Bill Smith)
Talks with Jackie Washington (with Jackie Washington)

EDITOR OF

17 Hamilton Poets
A Hamilton Anthology: Poetry
Image Fiction (with Gérard Dion & Margaret Strecker)
Dead Time: Poems from Prison

Recipes for Flesh

JAMES STRECKER

Mini Mocho Press

Hamilton, Ontario

A WORD OF THANKS

Thank you to the following, who in some way, large or small, encouraged this book to come into existence. In Canada: Margaret S., Ann T., Anne D., Vicki M., Marlene L., Michael S., JoAnne S., James A., Sharon F., Gérard D., Michael F., Joanna C., Kevin M., Bill S., Trudie T., Jean R. In the United States: Ira P., Isaac S., Doug M., Patrice G. In Europe: Chris M., Hans R., Chrissie H., Jeremy B., Martin C.

Published by Mini Mocho Press, Box 1138, Station A, Hamilton, Ontario, Canada L8N 4B3.

This limited edition of 1000 copies of *Recipes for Flesh* is published with the assistance of Chapman & Prince Booksellers.

ISBN 0-921980-01-9

CONTENTS

for Margaret
and for those
we love together

IN THE COTSWOLDS

The morning is a meadow
of stars, stars brought
home to rest in graces of
dew. The sheep seem riveted
to earth, grazing in the
fields overlapping from
town to town. It is
beautiful, too beautiful

for the traveller passing
by; he stops, enchanted,
in a music composed of
mounting celestial light
over sheep sparse as moons.
He feels his heart upside
down among the clouds; he
feels the meter of rain.

But his life is more a
butcher's art and he drives
home to eat the lamb he
hasn't killed, knowing the
sheep he left in pasture,
behind, are blood in his
blood, something akin to music.

DOCTOR TALK

The intern
describing a nurse
from Jamaica is
overheard: 'Once

you've had black meat,
you'll never want
white meat again.'

And the woman hearing this
becomes meat,

with meat, maybe cancer,
growing inside her belly.
She listens to the
specialist: 'We remove

the baby carriage but
you still keep the playpen.
It takes six months to heal.'

She listens to learn
that her body is her life,
listens forever alone
while fear and reassurance

numb the air
and the nothing in him
speaks to nothing in her.

PORPHYRY

As Porphyry advised
Firmus, his friend,
to abstain again
from meat's hypnotic
spell, so I advise you

too: consume a gentler
diet and reascend the
'realm of the Real'

and purify, approaching
gods, your soul of
forcign nature. Remember
the time when sacrifice
was bloodless offering
of apple and wheat, and

gods desired thus of
man 'pure intellect and
impassive soul.' I echo
that man, become more

humane, nears the divine,
that animals reason too,
though unheard by man,
and urge you to heed
what Pythagoras described:

Bassarians who slaughter
bulls and consume, in
turn, the putrid flesh
of fallen enemies.

From the Pont des Arts
the Seine flows sovereign
to thinking, forked until
married once more past the
Ile St. Louis, forked like
the human heart's fibre that,
breathing in, wills a holy

compassion, then, choking
surprised at its mercy,
exhales a barbarous laugh
and toys with every cruelty,
homesafe again. On the Pont
des Arts I am caught in this
storm like a fool rainsoaked

in ideals, wet through my
skin and believing, no matter
that I grant no trust in
humankind. But standing
mouth agape, taken by lightning
that shapes a celestial dining
fork into Belleville and the

Marais, and decrees the birthplace
slum of Piaf and the mended
luxury of a king's Place des
Vosges both food for divine
appetite, I find it very hard
to describe what is actually
happening, to describe and

not only describe but half a
truth. I remember the Rembrandt
painting of this afternoon, The
Flayed Ox: a headless carcass,
stubs for limbs, oils thick as
flesh rendered into masterpiece.
It is a jewel of artifice

but we know the guts have
fallen elsewhere. We ask
what is true, the painting
or the animal. In Rue St.
Denis, men group together
safely in packs to avenge
their need of women, and,

glaring a contempt thicker
than all the Louvre's art,
stare endlessly at the doorway
whores. They hate women; they
need to hate women, even the
blonde whose face is a lonely
man's lonely dream, the blonde

rendered neon on rouge,
standing more beautiful than
intended in a hallway gilded
with piss. What is human in
this? Women bought and sold
near butcher shops where liver
and thigh and tongue decay

obscenely together, a nesting
cache for flies and food for
whores and pimps. Flesh uses
flesh, consumes it impassive
and glad: no meat of philosophy
in this, even in Paris where
worms, who chewed Descartes'

reason from his bones and belched
up a conclusion no man can endure,
are themselves a compost for
time. In the Quartier Latin, each
restaurant window offers an altar
of death, each part of anatomy
allotted a price: the pig's head

stares stupidly ahead while,
slice by slice, its flesh is
consumed, salad to follow. Who
will bind all these pieces of
flesh together again to make
one life, or these organs and
muscles into one jig saw puzzle

that breathes? On the Pont des
Arts I hear wine in its laughter
again, the laughter of men
dining at white tablecloths,
each man a cup of mortality that
will empty for all time. This
man lives aloud, singing decay,

eats flesh that screamed as man
himself shall scream to become
a putrid nothing to no one
and forever. Man loves his dogs
and cats, and, drunk in the
groin, he loves his women too,
loves that his dumbest

indifference rots into art to
fertilize ennui. But my thinking
tonight is meat, bloody in
every manifestation, and man
too, the user of woman and earth,
the killer of lamb and whatever
he knows of soul, is meat as well.

He is butchered with each day, his
blood dried to powder, his killer
killed in turn because he stood
still. It is very hard to describe
what is actually happening: the
rain clouds flow out of sight down
a heavenly river and the sky

overhead, luminous mockery
of night, is full of gracious
possibility, river-reflected
and reflected in the heart. But
I kill and you kill and the rain
was really acid falling down
to kill in its promise like a

lover. And our promises too,
all of them, are but a whistle
stop on the route to war of
wars to end all wars when one
of us will kill and all of us
die for it. But enough: the sun
has reappeared if only to set

and the city is what we are, a
cruel, grimy elegance too stupid
for love. In mediaeval alleyways,
freckled with canine turds and
smelling of urine under three
star cuisine, the whores' foreplay
glances belittle the hunger in

men. The ruin of spirit lies
scattered, and passion waits to
make an ass of us before it truly
dies. Let us savour this world and
hear the rain once more, heaven-sent
and gurgling, a river, below, with
semen and blood in a sewer.

Hôtel du Vieux Paris, 1987

The brave explorers
of Europe went looking
for spices: spices

preserve meat, say
our teachers of history.
But in truth these

searchers of old craved
aphrodisiac, for pepper,
cloves, and cinnamon

were said to make man
erect. Then the Indians
of Mexico were butchered

for chocolate, also an
aphrodisiac; gold in
wooden ships was a bonus

that school kids understand.
But chocolate was bitter
and the trade in sugar

and black slaves began,
all because this laughable
thing called man would

kill his brother and ruin
the earth to stand tall.

ANIMALS

Sunset belongs
to animals: they

know every darkness;
they weave the

language of shadows;
they echo sun in the

moon like response
to an echo responding.

At sunset I pay heed
to my wife; she lies

in her darkness bedded
with cats; she touches

her cats and lays hands
on everything I know.

And cats blend their
purring through her

dream and my own, a
dream that isn't sleep,

while colour goes blind
in the sun's impeccable

hue, and all is gift,
a blossom of night.

I tarred some of the dogs
and set fire to them. I
disembowelled others and

poured boiling water into
the cavity. I held their
paws over a blowtorch. I

crushed the testicles of
some male dogs. I broke all
the bones of their limbs.

I gouged out the eyes of
some dogs and scraped the
orbits. In others I

manipulated the intestines.
I poured ether into the
windpipe. I shot one with

a .38 pistol, another with
a .32 pistol. I manipulated
the kidneys of one dog, then

its liver, then I inflicted
a serious injury to one of
its kidneys, then I shot

it with a .32 pistol. I
used 148 dogs to study
surgical shock. I used

incomplete anaesthesia.
In this year of 1899,
George W. Crile, physician.

Condemn all of suffering
or hypocrites we stand.

If you will not condemn,
be silent with philosophy:

your words on words argue
compassion in one breath,
in another reason the

innocent to living hell.
In time your students of
logic become mere sausages

of reason, begging mercy
on their blood, then spewing
the logic murder has become.

So poetry too is a luxury:
it runs to the soul not the
darkness in humankind, and

takes the road of willing
courtesy; it shirks to break
down the lab or slaughterhouse

door. Would it be that poetry
carried a loaded gun; would it
be that a gun were the answer.

ELSA HAIKU

Joy Adamson house
where Elsa was beloved:
chairs of lion skins.

Let us retell the
fable of the noble beast.

The lion strangles or
suffocates its prey, a
long, agonizing death. Its

cubs most often die
abandoned and starved, or
killed by other lions.

The females hunt but the
male claims feeding first,

but most often the lion is
a scavenger, eating rotted
carcasses left by hyenas,

wild dogs, or disease. And
the myth that lions kill
only what they need for food

is a deadly lie to wildebeest
wantonly brought down to
feed vultures, not the lion.

But the lion commends no
deceit, claims no human
morality, no hindsight guilt

as he kills and kills and kills
more barbaric than ever. See
the Jew, the Pole, the Hungarian

mother, the harmless orphans
of France, all dying together
in urine, without air, in

cattle cars. Now see the
cattle dragged from their
young, dying suffocated

in equal agony. And the smoke
of Dachau belches heavenward,
yellow with the fat of

prisoncrs newly arrived like
cattle, or green with starved
and meatless remains, while

the stench above another
slaughterhouse rises soundless
to the eye, and the flesh

is not burned or buried
but given the name of meat.

I would not be a Jew
to face the smiling fangs of
humankind; the Holocaust

begins anew in every smile.
Nor would I be cattle where
the curse of mankind

holds dominion over the earth
and morality smells of
rotted flesh in the belly.

You who are nameless

Bless this fusion
of the wild deer's heart
and my breathing.

Give life in everything
that flows a rainbow
of holy blood among
the reachable stars.

Make woman and man divided
one love, a love that
holds the orbit of
planets together.

Make ocean kind in your
blessing, and the storm,
the wild storm, a
blessing too.

You who speak without speaking

Let me hear the sound
between sounds, the
heartbeat of grasses, the
marrow of rocks, the

marriage of substance
and nothing. Make knowing
a spirit and bless it.
Make wonder the pulse

of each hour. Make men
restrain their madness
and let them overreach
to a star beyond the

stars in their blood,
in their flesh made earth,
in their wonder.

Let branches weave
through my skin. Let
bark and chaff be my
shelter. Teach me to love

when I have loved and
cursed, and lead me back
to this world, to the
seed of my beginning.

Let the earth find echo
in the raven overhead
and let the raven's
plumage, feathers a

twin of midnight sky,
give wing and music to
sunrise everlasting.

My heart is still young,
my hunger for love. I
try not to kill, nor shelter
my skin in fur. I try not
to reason man's cruelty, book

in hand. Maybe anthropology
is true and man was a hunter
before he plowed the earth;
or maybe a shortage of food
made him hungry for blood.

Maybe the woman's society ate
berries, not flesh; maybe
man deems himself the 'chosen
one' because he fears to grow
limp and die. But man, as he

stands, is a killer out of
hand, of mercy inconstant, of
thinking decayed. And I know
two dreams haunt my sleep: in
one I love my kind and wait,

wait for him to curb his
savage art; in the other, I
despair that he tortures what
is holy to me, so I shoot him,
I shoot him in the face.

A BLOCK OF WOOD

The yard is busy
with chickens. The old man,
my grandfather, is a teller
of bedtime stories. He

selects a brown hen near
the coop and holds the frantic
bird, two legs made one, in
his muscular hand.

The stump of a tree is
a wild crisscross of scars
and then it is bloody.

Next day, the boy who
watched the killing remembers
a greasy soup on his tongue.
He stares into the block

of wood for something he can
understand, something more
real than a dead chicken's
head in a ditch. He will

never hide in the ditch
again from demons described
by a man who carries an axe.

In a Spanish abattoir
the novice matador takes time
to rehearse. He thrusts his
sword, again and again, through
the flesh of captive cattle

waiting to die. The matador
perfects his art; the cattle
take a long time to die; the
stab wounds overlap. At the

Running of the Bulls in Tecate,
Mexico, a bull foams, wild-eyed,
at the mouth. Young men on
horseback drag his weary body,
skin on gravel, to the corral.

The spectators poke him, pelt
him with bottles and rocks,
spit on his fear because he
hesitates, he hesitates to die.

So, Picasso, did you sketch the
bull made ready for the ring?
They beat him, hurled sandbags
on his spine, pushed Vaseline
into his eyes, injected his

lonely and battered fear with
sedative, ground his horns to a
blunted, harmless nerve. So,
Hemingway, did you smile and

applaud a thrice-repeated
ritual, the neck muscles
shredded with pic and lance,
the banderillos maiming each
shoulder until the bull was a

helpless foe to the matador's
childish elegance? Did you
describe a bull tormented to
his only death, drenched in

the bloody hue of national
sport? O, man of painting, man
of literature, mired in one-
sided manhood and a coward's
olé, and you thousands, thirsty

for a helpless enemy, you
thousands who claim the geometric
duende Lorca described, dare you
also claim the name of humanity

in this? I wish upon your macho
lie the pain you prescribe for the
bull, a darning needle driven hard
through your own testicles,
O, you bastards.

LOVE POEM

Has the world become old
or am I alone in this affair?

Each day, more and more, she
enters the animal kingdom. And
I, conceived in her mystery,

cannot tell what species I've
become. At dawn I look
through her, through a window

that never breaks. I cannot
tell what species I've become.

perhaps, as I believed,
the bird was too mangled
to live (truly these

cats we love are expert,
equal to human, at
mauling the wounded)

or perhaps, deep inside,
I dreaded wounds, and
could not forgive the

suffering, and hated
the sparrow's need of
tending in a day too busy

for pity: but I am only
my deeds, without prophet
or saviour to forgive

me. I remember the bird
frozen still, staring
through my eyes until

this very day, as I
brought the heavy shovel
down upon its skull.

I took the morning dew to bed
I washed my body with her hair
And on her skin my image read
A hunter, I, though she lay bare

I took the meadow to my bed
Her grasses quivered in my hand
Though she was green, her body bled
A hunter kills to know the land

I took the mountain to my bed
And lost my breath to walk her round
And oft I knew the world from her
But in her stone no meadow found

I took the twilight to my bed
When dew was parched and meadow grey
And carried meadow o'er the gun
Where antlers made of comets play

Yet none of earth was true to me
When, echoed earth, I sang with dew
For men of love to darkness flee
And sing of earth, twice blind anew

And this is my dread,
my bottom line:

fingers crushed,
knees a bloodied splinter,
two arms at the shoulder

severed from my breathing,
a saw through my genitals,
a number inked on my thigh,

my name and heartbeat divided,
my muscle in one belly,
my kidneys in another,

all flushed into sewage
as you eat and shit again,
while nothing of spirit in me

reaches you, a corpse eating
corpse without eyes.

Because the cow's
a machine to suckle

man, not its own, the
calf, newly born, is
taken away. If female,

it becomes another
machine, if male, anemic
meat. Because the new
mother gives milk for

only ten months, rebreeding
takes place maybe fifty

days after the calf is born,
the machine greased and
oiled, you might say. The

human hand is absent from
this: rubber cups, plastic
tubes, and vacuum pumps
extract the cow's milk.

Warm milk then flows
directly to refrigerated
tanks twice a day. The
operator needs only to

disinfect the udder, apply
suction cups to the teats,
and tend the machinery,
living or stainless steel.

Feeding and water appear
automatically, manure
removed with ease, without
stench. Gates open and close

by technological magic.
When production wanes,
the cow is sent to a
slaughterhouse, not

graded high enough for
steak or chops but ground

to hamburger for fast-food
chains. The cows who remain,
many cows, are chained
by the neck, on concrete

floors, for months on end.
The hen is also a machine,

beaks and toes clipped
away because even hens will
kill their own, if locked
in cages piled high. Male

chicks don't lay eggs, so
of course they are suffocated
in heavy-duty plastic bags.

The hens are confined to
automation when mature. Two
conveyor belts bring feed
and collect the eggs, an

easy task because the eggs
roll away from the hens
down slanted floors. They
are washed and graded,

packed and stored; even the
chicken droppings are
scraped away by automatic

will, untouched by hen
or man. After a year
and a half, the profits

each hen produces begin
to dwindle. Each hen,
like two hundred and fifty
million other living gears

in the system, have ground,
useless rust, to a halt.
They are made into soup

and other processed food.
There are no psychiatrists
at a factory farm, though
cows and hens and men are

mad or going crazy, only
spare parts to replace the
wheels that have broken

down, because these cogs,
both flesh and steel, are
nothing but replaceable.

YOU WHO COUNSEL REASON

You who counsel reason, know this:

there is no hope but the fibre
of night before soliloquy,

the endless breath preceding time,

the eye without a looking glass
when blood and darkness entwine
like matter of wind,

when love and death mate precipice
and all of mind beneath half moon
is quarter moon lit,

and trees stand rooted in want of light,

and dance is what we are, all we are,
and dance is the river of silence
from blood to blood, from fish to bird

in man, until one voice, one mad and
chanting voice, avows we are dead
in anything we kill, dead beyond

mind and separation, dead beyond the
passing master plan, though living

backslid to heartless stone, a
stone of no core but solitude, and
slave to sacrifice of flesh,

the spirit of flesh we never were.

TWO PHOTOGRAPHS

One is a cat,

numb in restraint
and slowly going crazy,

belly up, legs spread
out to each corner,

belly up, ready for
incision to its nerves:

you will never forget
how its eyes are pleading

to die. The other is
a woman, gagged into

silence, elbows tied
behind her and she is

armless, naked from her
pleading eyes to ankles

clamped down with bolts,
and her legs spread apart,

at centre page, to show
pussy that someone, a

neighbour next door, also
studies with a dagger.

THE CLAUDE BERNARD PLAQUE

On the Rue des Ecoles,
a concrete commemoration:

DE 1847 A 1878
CLAUDE BERNARD
PROFESSEUR DE MEDECINE
AU COLLEGE DE FRANCE
A TRAVAILLE DANS CE LABORATOIRE

Beside me the ghost of a dog
wonders aloud:

It must say that Claude Bernard
thought himself a great scientist
and no ordinary man. It must
say he felt possessed by scientific
ideas and refused to hear the
cries of animals or even see their
flowing blood. It must say
he took dogs for living machines
that he cut very slowly into pieces.

Not quite, I answer.

Then surely it describes how Bernard
cut open thousands of animals,
destroyed an organ in each one, and
kept them alive for hours prolonged
and prolonged without anaesthesia,
and how he was mimed in cruelty
in labs all over Europe.

Well no, I answer.

Does it say that Bernard's
teacher, Magendie, immobilized
a small cocker spaniel by
driving nails through its paws
and long ears in order, without
anaesthetic, to saw open the
living dog's cranium and dissect
its spine to expose raw nerves,
and left the puppy, not yet dead,
for use the next day?

It doesn't mention Magendie, I reply.

Does it mention how Bernard, member
of the Académie Française and hero
to France, advocated in private,
without qualm, the vivisection
of human beings, while he continued
to roast living rabbits and dogs
in an oven to their death?

That too isn't here, I respond.

Then what in hell does it say? asks
the ghost of a dog.

It says he worked in this lab
for 31 years.

Paris, 1987

THE MORNING OF CONVERGENCE

A day of
universal love

yet these seekers
of grace

would eat
human flesh

and still ask
for the recipe

The dinner talk has turned literary,
quotation passing for wisdom. I stare

into the trees for words, words that
step aside like worldly gentlemen to
let a windy pretension pass by, words
that carpet the forest like cicada
sound, words of truth and ecstasy. I am

seeking a solitary branch, one holding
a forest of leaves and my meaning. I
am seeking words that are leaves because
I surrendered some borrowed ideas long
ago. One idea flowed into another, and

my thinking, a snow-laden branch, fell
down, broken from the earth. I spoke
ideas I had learned and they cracked,
heavy with craft and reason, even as
the sun played magnet to earth and my

thinking grew back on the trees and the
sky was again a kind of literature.
I can tell you how leaves rot into decay.
I can tell you that fur, like scale or
skin, sings echo to leaves. Or how

I hope against reason that some leaves
will never die. But words are words,
only words, when spoken too easy, too
wise, too broken from the heart. I can
tell you this: These words eating

flesh, these words wanting flesh, must
die and decay for new leaves to grow.

TEMPLES

On vacation one decade apart,
my two friends Raymond and Bob,

both home from Oriental temples
seasoned with millennium, temples

washed porous and clean of holy war
and bloody, holy daggers, temples

carved sacred for Hindu, Buddhist,
and Jain, and gods of every hour,

speak only of temples overlooking
classy restaurants where inside they

sew the lips of a living monkey
together, push its skull through a

hole at centre table, saw off the
skull's crown, and sip the fluids of

the live monkey's brain through a straw,
all for the pleasure of a delicacy.

ELEGY

You are not alone
in this:

>>   to ease
the rotted pain
of your dying cat

you paid a doctor
for shooting a deadly
poison into its blood,

and then, where no one
might see you crack in
two, you cried and cried,

and traded all of humanity
for something that loved
and touched you more

WHAT DID YOU EAT?

What did you eat
this evening?

The limb of a calf
that never saw light

and stood in one place
unable to turn

each morning the
birthday of nothing

for ninety-five days
till you cooked its

anemic flesh and
prayed over dinner to

a god who might save
your children from

a cruel indifference
such as yours.

In Nairobi, a Hilton hotel
pampers the rich. Two
Kenyan brothers are divided,
one jetted over his native
and rain-starved earth to
study computers Ivy League,

and the other tending cattle
at seven, fated to die a
statistic before he becomes
a man. Who can tell how the
fabric of spirit weaves
through each one, leaving a

raw mortality behind? Who
can say each kneels to gods,
kneels to learn there is no
deity? Above, the sky mates
endless time and, cloudless,
milks their thinking and mine

as I stand in Masai Mara and
shiver in awe of my very own
heart, in awe that my heart
knows willingly how to die.
Do I matter in this world of
mysteries? Or have I become

too wise for God, for happiness,
for the very sperm I carry?
Each day I get drunk on illusion
to forget what I am, a man of
mundane dread who eats and
defecates, knowing this day

at hand might be a marker
on his grave. But this
gazelle, dead and miles
from no one, will claim no
marker to adorn its going,
only bones and a skull that

wants to blush, seeming shy
to be naked of skin. Why must
the dead smell? Or tolerate,
with lungs still full of air,
bowels full of grass, these
vultures immune to anything

of grace, sticking, one by one,
a hooked and hungry beak up
the dead gazelle's ass? In
Nairobi, the alley boxes are
full of tin cans thrown away,
but can we dispose of the mortal

joke we are? We of five and dime
gods who still die? We who might
screw out our brains and still
die? Give me your learning: we
need to matter though we don't.
The ice of our laughter makes

us liars to say we might be
happy. Have we not gone mad to
love this world? Have we not
sung puny repertoires, made
learning deceit, spiked power
with a coward's art, killed

like false omnipotent gods
in dread to be lost for a
moment and forever? Have we
not taken partners in crime,
fellow sinners to blaspheme
the flicker of beauty

furrowed in our genes? Have we
not become inept and scarred
to the gods we aspired to be?
But watch this foul repast
cleanse the earth of a thing
that knew the sun more elegant

than we. The gazelle killed no
flesh to sidestep its own, absurd,
end; it burned no woman or child
alive, augmented no unspeakable
pain to make silence of its own.
It ran these infinite grasses

like a branch with evening wind
veined inside its bark, one of
millions that mattered godless
and untallied, that mattered
nonetheless because miracles
count for something. Shall we

name our kind a miracle? This
human thing that hates its
reflection and curses, in deed,
all mankind, that finds freedom
in making wounds, that analyzes
love? What salvation, born Jesus,

can remedy the ruin of being
alive, the pain of being
nothing and alive? In the
jargon of efficient men, fear
is mere inconvenience, a malady
that keeps us from getting on

with the job. And perhaps we
are stupid, not evil, a thing
that screws its own image, a
thing aimed at heaven that
smells. Here vultures blanket
the dead gazelle; it is lost

forever to talons of steel.
And miles from this lousy death
good Canadian citizens kill time
with their humanity; they watch
each living masterpiece pale to
nothing beside their love.

Nairobi & Hamilton

When I touch my cat
a miracle takes hold
beneath my fingertips,

skin on fur one element,
one breath of air.

Still we can do nothing
but watch sometimes, as
all we love is wounded in

spirit or flesh, or gives
wounds. So we wonder that

love is a feast for the
lonely and dreaming, a
feast with a portion
of razors on the side.

SHOPPING LIST

In Toronto's Chinatown
you can buy
the gallbladder of a bear,

an aphrodisiac, say the ancients,

while the carcass of this bear,
with a thousand of its kin,
rots for a couple of dollars
in the wilderness.

You can buy
the shiny pelt of a fox
while a hunter digs his heel
through the gullet of another,
or clubs its head to mush,

or, risking blood on his prize,
turns its neck with a shepherd's crook,
and shoots the footless victim,
a bullet through the eye.

You can buy
the skin of a wolf,
run down to exhaustion by ski-doo
or hunted with walkie-talkie
from the frozen air above.

And government shall not offend,
and says nothing;
and we shall not offend,
and say nothing....

plus ça change....
ex nihilo nihil fit.

YOU CALL ME NAIVE

as you defend vivisection,

your neighbour punches the
face of his wife to a pulp,

he buggers his child daughter,

and his belly is full of a thousand
animals that died in mechanical pain.

as you defend vivisection,

a pilot drops napalm on schoolyards,
gas in the lungs of cities far away,

a soldier burns peasant genitals with
voltage enough to light a starving town,

a president stockpiles the world's end
for corporate payola, for God he says.

but when man the scientist enters a lab,
you claim, he becomes a creature of moral

finesse, a man who carves his own heart
in the victim he maims, not a man who

enjoys the helpless tied down while
his hunger to wound hears nothing,

nothing of eyes that scream.

Darkness.
The branches overhead entwine.

Beyond the branches entwining
more branches; each ending
is root to another.

The earth below is a web
of gnarled roots, the trees
around me the texture,
the silence of bark.

And these, my two hands, hold
together around the scent
of pine, my unwilled instinct
for prayer cupped in these fingers.

I am random in this happiness:
everything is new. At length of my
arm away, a chipmunk sits wary
and frozen, awaiting the predator's

hand I might deal. Beyond the trees
a daylight of eyes squints to kill
what it sees, where clouds overhead
entwine like fingers around the sun.

My mother has wept
forty years, over
a sow she and my
father butchered
one autumn for meat.

She knows and despairs
by reading and looking
around that human
art is to torture
what is helpless,
tied down. But

chemotherapy has
deprived her of any
taste for food; she
can stomach neither
biscuit nor water
so she starves.

To live, says the
family physician, she
needs to force meat
down her throat, so
meat she eats. And she
feeds the starlings

through winter, while
eating the hens she
would shelter in a kinder
world, while choking on a
sow that died for her plate
like a curse on her tears.

The year is 830 A.D.
A new calendar shows man
the master, harvesting

where he chopped the spirit
of trees in two, lukewarm
in pity to the pigs he

slaughters for meat, shows
nature the servant and man
the guiding hand of all

his god has left for man
undone. Eight centuries
ahead, a passage in the

Oeuvres of Descartes denies
the animals' jagged cry of
pain, hears only a rusty,

mechanical noise, like a
wheel, like a creaking hinge,
and gives torture a rational

blessing. The year is 1969
and Dachau seems an eerie,
vacant stage between scenes.

Are there words, any words,
to describe these photographs?
Doctors did their job. A

tourist beside me is appalled
that rabbits and white mice
were discarded for Polish

priests and peasants from the
Ukraine. When is life no
longer a life, no longer

worthy of mercy? I wonder
half aloud. But I know
she would rather be kin to

a Nazi butcher, than find
her worth akin to rabbits
and mice, no more nor less

esteemed in rot or dust. So
I buy the guidebook souvenir
and wait for my train in a

restaurant where the smoke
of dead flesh, like any flesh,
flows rancid into tomorrow.

I could not see Terry Fox
hopping by, on his run
for cancer research. The

air was too polluted with
gaseous fumes and metal
dust, too thick with poison
vapours that keep our

livelihoods burning and
spike us with cancer. And
most of our citizens were
too busy to cheer this

gutsy young man anyway: The
kids were downing hamburger
with the works, meaning
chemicals they couldn't

pronounce; the populace was
smoking its collective lungs
to a cancerous rot; and
research scientists were

seeking another wonder drug
to bless disease the hunger
for money had wrought, like
Thalidomide, or Cyclophosphamide,

or Oxychinol, or some other
miracle researched cure that
kills in the name of healing.

at heart, creation
is compassionate,
compassion creative,

the one a fuse of love
to all it surveys, a
maker remaking the
earth, the other

a flame of merciful awe
through every wretched
madness of this world:

beside the coffin of
Glenn Gould, his aunt
describes how the pianist,
companion in music to Bach,

in unspoken hymn to animals,
had founded in his dream
a farm where cows bound
for slaughter might live

out their lives in peace,
hermit though one with
the earth, like the pianist
lying here, with pasture

for piano beyond the cruel
cacophony of men who
cannot make love their art.

Not three square meals
a day, with a portion
of flesh, that schools
recommend, because they
abide the meat profiteers,
and not the smiling fool
of a cartoon tuna dragged
from its home, the sea,
and not cartoon hot dogs
seducing your young to a
guiltless fantasy on
Saturday morning TV, and
not the 'turkey juices'
that grandpa, the pacifier,
carves on Thanksgiving,
or the sizzling barbecue
that macho, suburban dad
provides to feed his kids,
all would-be men, and not
the movie celebrity, a
legend wearing fur in
yuppie magazines, the
superstar paid in millions
who makes a killing twice,

but you who pay the killer
to bloody his hands, while
you chip in bucks for the
SPCA, and, full in the
belly with the dead you
would not hear, you weep
real tears for Bambi.

LUNCH

My friend has ordered
a nitrite hamburger,
bloodless remains the colour
of rouge when her teeth get
inside. This is Yonge Street:

fast food and faster sex door
to door. We remember an Asian
girl of ten, the height of a
plastic doll she might carry,

sold with her lifetime as a
blowjob machine. If lucky, she
is dead. But she has sisters,
grainy and underexposed in a

basement cinema next door.
Says my friend, 'A woman is
nothing but a piece of ass in
this male society.' And she

watches the hustlers hang out,
the middle class kids from
suburbia, and the signs that
promise sex for the hopeless.

And her thoughts drift over
the stench of burning flesh,
to a place where, sick of heart
and sick of men, she dines on
steak in a kinder world.

In a hospital
where the meat
of one dinner

is recycled
into hash
for the next
day's meal,

clearly nothing
of flesh is
wasted; I

awaken, one of
many, after
surgery, and
shudder to

discover my
belly is
stapled
together.

If we go full tilt with mercy
who vows that earth will be kind?
There is no end of darkness, no
ember of eternal light. And each
man remembers in dying he was
born someone else, born a sun to

die a rancid star. He remembers
the ruin love made, a ruin echoed
in his heart, as the earth claims
his age and flows in muted secrecy,
year by year, upward into blossom
over his open grave. Yet shall

we never walk among the dreams
of other men, before the flowers
bloom from their outstretched hands,
and show in their nightmare prison
how colours of love might hang
green on green together? This world

of ghostly persuasion bleeds mad
into time, where stars fall like
snow and we wish, poor simpletons we
are, that our fall might have been
easier. Still I dream the midnight
of a second star when men, unashamed

of their mercy, find love the fibre
of man to confess, to wager, to
harvest and plant again. And stronger
the dream, then stronger the fibre,
then brighter the fibrous light we
call love. Dare we swear upon this

light that kindles the dream
that has made it? Dare we pray
from every hypocrisy for the
killer to eat his own flesh, then
pardon the earth, his body, for
a rooted and meaningless end?

They inch together
and pose for photographs,

and prove, one day to remember,
they stood side by side, one
thing with one smile. Are

they actors, miles divided though
arm in arm, naked yet never naked
for each other? The male eats

meat and sweats his dinner, an
odour she despises. He hunts with
a rifle and kills, from afar,

what she, alone, would save. She
refuses to eat the flesh he has
killed; he reminds her that

'carrots have feelings too.'
So she turns to the wisdom of her
guru who consoles her to sleep
with these words: 'If love is

all, then all of this is love. If
God is all, then all of this is
God.' She reads this wisdom from
afar, like a hunter taking aim,

until she snores a dream and
remembers, dreaming, what she's
hocked for happiness.

A VEGETARIAN DINES WITH ACADEMICS

I don't eat meat on moral grounds.

AQUINAS, AQUINAS

I stopped one day when I held a raccoon
in my hands and decided in a flash that
no animal should die because of my diet.

KANT, KANT

I think man should rethink his very
nature, and consider himself but an atom,
not a ruler, of earth and universe.

NIETZSCHE, NIETZSCHE

Yes I know man does evil, evil beyond words,
but despair of the cynic is a coward's path
and man must learn to dignify himself with
compassion, or else he's but a moral poseur.

DOSTOEVSKY, DOSTOEVSKY

I know that animals kill most cruelly too,
but a species that claims to chew the fat
with gods must think and act apart.

DARWIN, DARWIN

But enough of mankind. How shall we explain
the ways of animals?

DISNEY, DISNEY

BLOOD

I heed no magic
but the music of living blood,
this finite conjuration,
holy for all time,
transformed from common, red water
to a pulse of bottomless hours.

Who are you to mouth what you've heard
while magic suspends me, water to chin,
in the fusion of everything alive?
Who are you to divide the blood
of human and ape, and torment
the artwork of gods?

I own no book to verify
the soul of gorilla or chimpanzee,
or proof that baboon would indeed be
kinder than man (though many a stone
can mime the human heart). But the
chain of being is a braggart's joke
when my kinship with the ape
hurls a planet through me.

DESIRE

The fur you wear
has no feet; the
fox, in a trap,

chewed its foot
to the bone, then
died a long death,
its vein a faucet

on snow. The shoes
you wear are the
skin of a calf
who lived a conveyor
belt life. Without

mother or touch
of any kind, it
reached for a nipple

and was fed a
chemical gruel. Your
lipstick was force-fed
down the gullets
of mice and rats

until their stomachs
distended in agony;
your powder filled

beagle stomachs until
they burst. Even your
shampoo was dripped

into rabbits' eyes
until they went
blind and crazy
in a bolted vice.

Now if you undress,
I'll desire you.

For a moment
I'll go crazy in
your smell and follow
each strand of your
hair to the moon

beyond the moon.
But then I'll vomit
on your perfumed
skin, because

you've become all
that died for
your beauty.

In a holding tank
for the helpless,
the severely retarded,

with less than monkey
IQs, are strapped into
beds until they die.

Down Main Street, the
foetus of a teenage
pregnancy is suctioned,

piece by piece, into
garbage. At a fast
food hamburger

restaurant between the
two, a steer, confused
by traffic driving by,

is made to pose like
a toy for photographs.
No doubt, the decent

souls, troubled by some
of this, will boil a
lobster to death at lunch.

It's a summer
I can hardly remember

though August remains
borne aimless and parched
above the Catskill Mountains
and the Hudson flowing south.

The sunset does fiery tricks
all around, cocky in crimson,
cocky in gold, and waits to
speak the last word while
daylight dozes off.

I too would linger afire,
be one with oneness, and still
not extinguish my inner fire
by wanting to linger.

These mountains I travel
rise and fall with my breathing,
still green in the curvature
of time, and I know the unseen

deer have spoken one silence,
a silence known by all who are
deer and man, a silence heard
as it flows, like blood, in
the dread we know together.

I can say this or be still,

for nothing that is can truly be.
All perfections of mountain
and sun are gathered within us
to wither. I know they wither;

sunset passed through me
before. The sunset passed
through me, I knew nothing

but sun, sun and perfection
that sunset allows. But the
world, in being, was already
something else, something

afire in the part of me that
dies. I could not name the
fire: I found love, made love,
in my sleep and dreaming

between suns, made love as I
died. Did I know I would die
in this mangled deer at
roadside, its dead tongue,

like my tongue, hanging parched
and fallen toward the sun, the
sun still afire in paradise
leaves yet forever dead?

Stony Point, August 1987

In a moment,
a split hair of time,

the dog that yelped and clawed
its remnant dignity
becomes merely a thing bolted down,

a silent thing too, numbered on a
chart, that man who severed its
vocal chords will now carve and maim.

Still you can find justice, balance
of a kind: man with science or god
to bless this cruelty is no less
a devil to his kind. And, granted,

the earth makes an inside joke of
man, seems to laugh in compensation.
Thus the vivisectionist, for one,
knows a special kind of hell: Claude

Bernard, a schizophrenic and manic
depressive at the end, or his
colleague Blanchard who, blind,
sees ghostly eyes of cats he has

tortured, who, dying out of reason,
implores his family to remove the
eyes of cats surrounding his bed. Or
Flourens, successor to the esteemed

Bernard, roaming his final days in
the Jardin des Plantes, howling and
barking like the dogs of his
laboratoire. Or John Read, cancer in

his nerves, the very nerves he has
poked in living dogs, who writes,
'This is a judgement on me for the
pain I have inflicted on animals.'

But we are not the earth, you and
I, but men like all men who are
given speech to say nothing. Dare
we presume in sanctuary of art

to balance the maddening pain of
dogs and cats? Dare we feign to be
wise? But what wisdom is there, what
rage, to number the animals, 200

million, dead in labs this year
around the earth, this very earth
that grants us poetry? And you
with kin raped and starved in

concentration camps, you know
spine-deep how slowly men torture
for their god, their science, their
master race, while they claim a

mountain of sacrifice to save the
rest of us. Keep sane and read
these figures: 4,221,801 experiments
on living animals, British licence,

1983. How exactly did they test
pesticides 32,979 times? Or what
new medical miracle gave moral
balance to the killing of 932,335

rats? What colour were the 251,818
birds a nameless, unguarded someone
used with law on his side? And
what do psychological stress,

burning and scalding, electric
shock, or interference with the
brain and parts of the central
nervous system mean to you? Do

you shudder and cry aloud for
these lives in poems that mirror
your own pain? Do you see yourself
tied down in a lab, nameless

like your tormentor, pleading for
death not pity of a man who
cannot hear, of a man who seeks a
cure for every disease and, being

even a man who reads poetry,
cannot cure himself because he calls
himself sane and enjoys his lunacy?

COMMUTING

This morning I
commuted to work
beside a livestock
truck. The trailer's
side was a wall of
metal and pinkish
skin. Pigs this
time: a snout without

eyes squeezed through
an air hole, inhaling
its first and last
morning in one. The
trailer's rubber tires
whirred a rapid 'schnell,
schnell, schnell' on
the QEW, and the CBC

news was a drone of
editorial concern: war
in Latin America, war
in the Persian Gulf, and
maybe, as ever, an
impending nuclear war.
For a second I imagined
the pig walking free,

rummaging for food in
a sty big as the earth,
pushing human remains
aside with a curious
and eager snout, in
search of an edible
meal below piles of
sizzling, human skin.

We come upon hunters at twilight.
They carry traps and hatchets,
flaunt a predator's private joke
in their smiles, and drunk with beer
or killing (I cannot tell) point,

satisfied, at their prize: coyote and
muscrat, heads askew, with eyes like
jewels in a crown of death. And the love
inscribed in a forest-height of books,
the everlasting gods of mercy that

man, time-born, conceives, the hours
of woman and man when summer sings
reason to dance, become a holy blessing
held in dirty hands. And if you are
not cursed, I curse you, killers of this

beauty, this innocence, for even upon
the blood-thirsty earth we wander, lost,
without meaning, together, both beauty
and mercy endure, married as one. But
my curse is a mirror held in my enemy's

name, and I would not ask to dream what
makes me mad: something of flesh, like
by body, is a killer; something of
flesh, like my body, is dead. Yet if
the choice for blood ran a balance of

justice through time, and if the choice
of life or life were my own, I would
hang each hunter's throat to the moon,
till this muscrat and coyote ran, living,
to a haven over darkness, over man.

Le Coupe-Chou restaurant
is the site of a barbershop
buried under fear, in legend,

a barbershop whose happy proprietor
slit the throats of his customers
with a razor and without last rites.

His equally happy neighbour
was a butcher who, wasting not, made
human remains into a voguish pâté.

Le Coupe-Chou was closed the day
I walked by, but as I peered through
a window, I saw my body spread out

and decomposing along a warm and crusty
baguette, a bier and a plat du jour
for a Michelin gourmet.

I should have known as well
that birds decay in autumn,
fallen like too many leaves.
And that winter is the season

we hold in our genes, when the
dead look up to touch the
underside of snows and wonder
in their perfect way if we, who

tally the seasons, might ever be
happy. I should have known we
were nameless in our names, and
our dreams unmarked graves,

though we claimed a wisdom,
a kind of mystery. We followed
the geese flying south to the
edge of winter, and knew the

stars paid attention. But who
knows what the stars really think
those millions of light years
away where we count for nothing

but our dreaming. I know, I
surely know, I wonder to be
alive, this said while mountains
of authorless leaves crack the

shell of my wonder. To love is
to lose and I carry my dead; yet
the dusty ruin lying here still
gives my heart the voltage of stars.

Death mated hard with
the sun, turned the season
of roses to a shroud, worked
our mere, human reason with
callused, icy hands. The
shelter beauty allows betrayed
us in his death, for he,
companion of timeless art,
was made mortal and ended.
And the art, the painting and
sculpture he touched with
love, touched with awe the
very soul of love, flickers,
a candle in darkness now,
if beauty betrays. Still
he was a planter of seeds,
a seller, with Vincent his
cat, of spirit made craft,
who, spirit in man, took
wasteland for a garden, made
it grow. And he was a friend,
his life a gentle life, an
unassuming masterpiece of
gentleness. May his art, his
very life, echo firm in our
deeds; may we know, as he
knew, how the only good of
this world is the kindness
we, in darkness born, take
quiet, everyday courage to be.

August 19, 1988

Do not enchant the dead
how we matter,
or cover their ruin
like spring, false spring.

Our dreams sing loud
the song of our flesh,
so loud to ache,
so loud not to waken us.

We die by their will,
forever unborn, as godless
with gods, like sound,
their hearts eternally perish.

And father, forget them,
for they know what they do.
They have killed, are killing,
what is mother of god in you.